Ladybird 🐞 Readers

Big Bad Bash

Series Editor: Sorrel Pitts
Story by Catherine Baker
Illustrated by Ian Cunliffe

Ladybird Readers Starter Level

Title		Phonics	Sight Words
1	Alphabet Book	A—Z	
2	Is it Nat?	s a t p i n	a is it
3	Nat Sits		an in sit
4	Top Dog and Pompom	m d g o c k	and can I into no
5	Top Dog is Sick		got not
6	The Fun Run	e u r h b f l	at get go has off the to up
7	Gus is Hot!		full his of on put
8	Jazz the Vet	j v w x y z qu	be but had he him she tell was
9	Vick the Vet		did well will
10	Dash and Thud	ch sh th ng	if ran then they with yes
11	Big Bad Bash		big long that this
12	The Big Fish	ai ee oa oo	her look see them
13	The Big Ship		let me my too
14	Martin and Lorna	ar or ur ow oi er	all are for
15	Farmer Carl		cut down good help now
16	The Big Dipper	igh ear air ure	as have like said some went you
17	The Silver Ring		come from so stop we what

First, go through the phonemes on page 4, and do the activity on page 5. Then, read the words in the first half of the book, focusing on pronunciation and blending.

The sight words are introduced in the second half of the book, first on their own and then in full sentences.

At the back of the book, there are activities and assessments practicing phonemes and sight words. These icons indicate the key skills required in each activity:

 Spelling and writing   Speaking   Reading

Big Bad Bash

Look at the story

First, look at the words and pictures.
Use the words to practice phonics.

Phonics focus

ch   sh   th   ng

Dash

Bash

the long thing

thud

thick muck

chop

Aa Bb Cc Dd Ee Ff Gg Hh Ii Jj Kk Ll Mn

Activity

1 Look. Say the sounds.
Write the letters. 📖 🗨 ✏

| sh | ch | ng | sh |

1 Da sh

2 lo

3 op

4 Ba

Bash

Dash   thick muck

the long thing

Bash

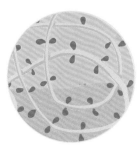

the long thing

Dash

the long thing

12

thick muck

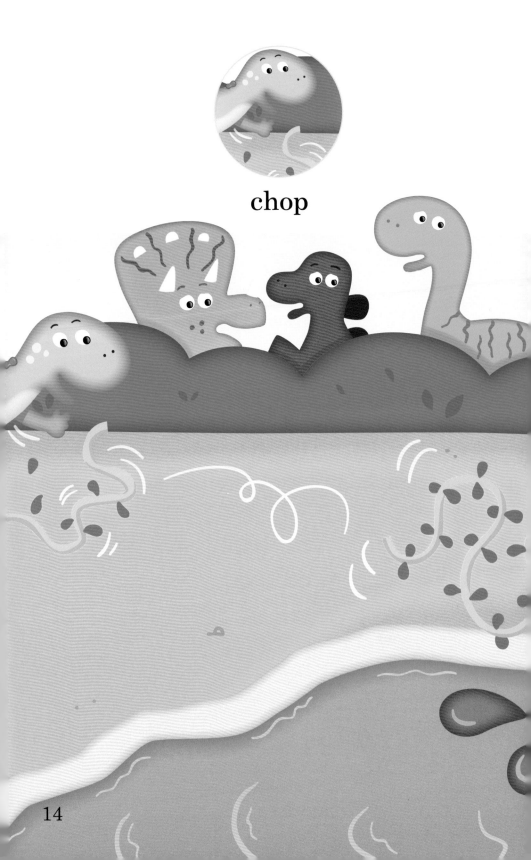

chop

thick muck

15

Big Bad Bash

Read the story

Now, read the story in full sentences.
Practice using the sight words.

Sight words

big

long

that

this

17

Bash was big and bad.

I can chuck Dash into that thick muck.

Then, Dash got a long thing.

Bash hung on to the
long thing.

22

23

Dash ran off to a big bush.

I can fix this long thing on to the bush.

24

Bash had to tug and tug.

Dash chops the long thing.

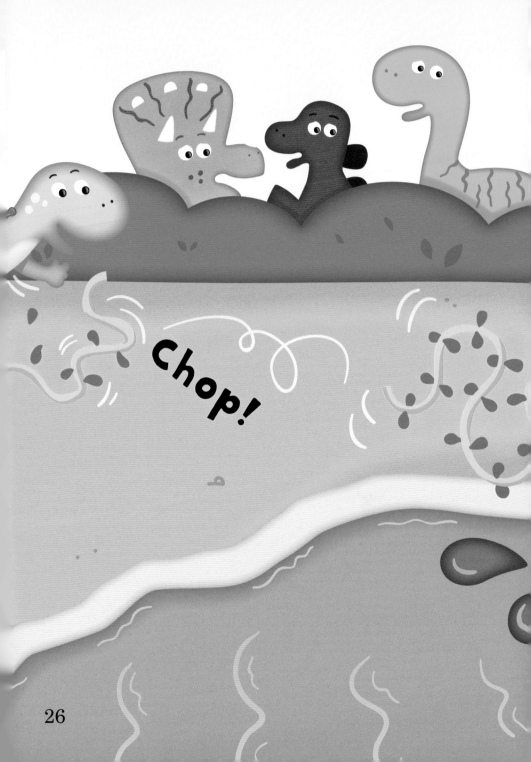

26

Bash fell into the muck
with a thud!

Activities

2 **Say the words. Draw the pictures and color them in.** 🗨 📖

Dash got a long thing.

Bash fell into the thick muck!

3 **Find the sight words.**

long

this

big

that

c h l p n g long e f g w t h i s o t u y b i g o k t t h a t s f d t

Assessment

4 **Look and read. Match.**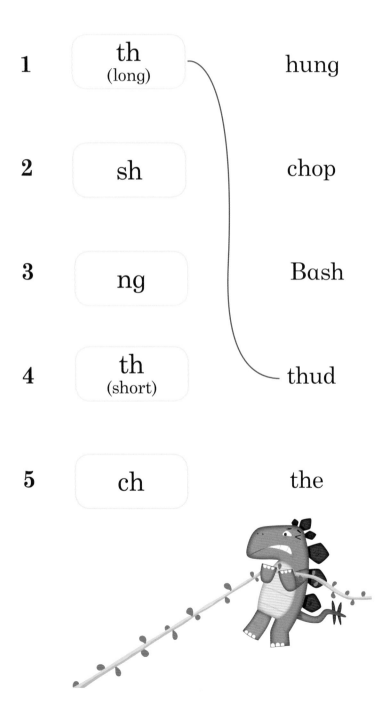

1	th (long)	hung
2	sh	chop
3	ng	Bash
4	th (short)	thud
5	ch	the

5 Say the sight words. Write them on the lines. 📖 💬 ✏️

big	long	this	that

1

Bash is _big_ and bad.

2

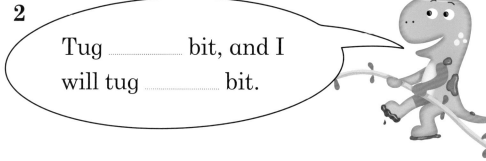

Tug _____ bit, and I will tug _____ bit.

3

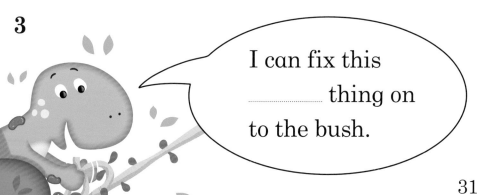

I can fix this _____ thing on to the bush.

Starter

Starter 1	Starter 2	Starter 3	Starter 4	Starter 5
Alphabet Book	Is it Nat?	Nat Sits	Top Dog and Pompom	Top Dog is Sick
978–0–241–39367–3	978–0–241–39368–0	978–0–241–39369–7	978–0–241–39370–3	978–0–241–39371–0
Starter 6	Starter 7	Starter 8	Starter 9	Starter 10
The Fun Run	Gus is Hot!	Jazz the Vet	Vick the Vet	Dash and Thud
978–0–241–39372–7	978–0–241–39373–4	978–0–241–39374–1	978–0–241–39375–8	978–0–241–39376–5
Starter 11	Starter 12	Starter 13	Starter 14	Starter 15
Big Bad Bash	The Big Fish	The Big Ship	Martin and Lorna	Farmer Carl
978–0–241–39377–2	978–0–241–39379–6	978–0–241–39380–2	978–0–241–39381–9	978–0–241–39382–6
Starter 16	Starter 17			
The Big Dipper	The Silver Ring			
978–0–241–39383–3	978–0–241–39384–0			

LADYBIRD BOOKS

UK | USA | Canada | Ireland | Australia
India | New Zealand | South Africa

Ladybird Books is part of the Penguin Random House group of companies
whose addresses can be found at global.penguinrandomhouse.com.
www.penguin.co.uk   www.puffin.co.uk   www.ladybird.co.uk

Penguin
Random House
UK

First published 2017. This edition published 2019
001

Copyright © Ladybird Books Ltd, 2017

Printed in China

A CIP catalogue record for this book is available from the British Library

ISBN: 978-0-241-39377-2

All correspondence to:
Ladybird Books
Penguin Random House Children's
80 Strand, London WC2R 0RL